Social Media Strategies for Small Businesses

Table of Contents

Introduction

Social media is one of the most dominant forms of communication in the digital space. It has drastically altered the traditional relationship between a consumer and a business.

I learned this the very hard way…I paid $3.5K for a website that 3 months after it was finished, I could not manage, update or change.

Every time I made a call to my "web guy", I was out $150 and unhappy with the results. Something had to give.

I had learned that blogging was important for my business. I didn't know why but all I remember is that it was good for SEO. S-E-Whaaa? Yeah…I had no clue!

I began to blog. I blogged about my frustrations as an entrepreneur. Ok I complained….A LOT. But then I decided to do something about it. Armed with my 10-month old child, a Mac Book and a kick-ass internet connection, I set out to make WWW -and my website- mine.

I blogged even more, I asked questions, I took courses, webinars, read books and finally, I got certified.

I am not going to tell you I am the best thing since Latin Java (whatever that is), although that does sound pretty nice! What I will tell you is that I've done the work. I've researched, I've implemented, I've invested time, energy and resources in these strategies not just for myself, but for my clients. Almost 9 years and I'm still in business, so grateful for every second of it!

All joking aside, here's what I can also tell you: It is important that as a modern professional you have some knowledge of how Social Media works and affects you and your business. It's also important that you know how to leverage this marketing channel to grow your online presence, business and to also protect your reputation.

This guide offers you a solid foundation to understand social so you can plan, execute, and assess effective social media campaigns. I know it will be helpful.

With that said, let's roll!

Social Media Questionnaire

Here are a few questions to get you started.

1. Who is your target audience?

_____

_____

2. What are your current goals? (S. M. A. R. T. Goals template attached)

_____

_____

3. What are your biggest challenges?

_____

_____

4. Who are your competitors?

_____

_____

5. Who do you admire on social media?

_____

_____

6. What is your quarterly budget for social media?

_____

_____

7. What are you currently doing on social media that's working well?

_____

_____

8. How much time do you have to dedicate to social media every week?

_____

_____

How to Set Your SMART Marketing Goals

Whether you have short-term or long-term goals, this planning template[1] can help you manage the process. The template will help you clearly describe your goals, set a deadline for meeting them, and understand the desired end result. This will all be accomplished by focusing on **SMART**, a methodology that helps you make "smart" goals! Before jumping to the template, let's review what SMART stands for.

Specific
When creating a goal, you want it to be as short, crisp, and specific as possible. Having "a good marketing year" isn't a reflection of what your company actually accomplished. Imagine that your boss is about to leave for vacation, and you have less than 90 seconds until he/she runs out the door, and all they want is to quickly hear what next year's goal is -- what are you going to tell him or her that concisely explains your plans?

Measurable
Oftentimes, companies say they want to "increase their social media following." While that is a goal, it's not a trackable goal. If you start the new year with 100 followers, and end with 101, technically you met your set goal. But if you switch that goal to read, "We want to increase social media following by 25%," suddenly you can measure your progress every month to see if you're on track to ultimately jumping from 100 to 125 followers. Now you really know you hit your goal -- hopefully it's more ambitious than this example!

Attainable
While having history-breaking goals are beneficial it's still important to keep these goals realistic. If in your company history you've generated an average of 10 leads every month, jumping to 2,000 leads per month would be a drastic change. Many businesses do this to push employees and to "go as far as they possible can." But in reality, this can be discouraging, as you can never actually be successful. SMART goals are goals you can actually achieve.

Relevant
Why have a goal if the goal doesn't matter? Say you're a teddy bear business that, at maximum, can only sell 1,000 teddy bears per month. In this situation, your goal likely shouldn't be to "increase production of teddy bears from 1,000 per month to 5,000 per

---

[1] Adapted from HubSpot.com

month." While it's great you have more product, if your existing distributors won't buy more, why bother? Your goal should be something along the lines of, "increase distribution channels by X%."

Time-Bound

While having all the aforementioned helps develop a solid goal, you need to ensure you have a timeline for meeting that goal. Going back to the teddy bear example, if you do decide your goal is to increase distribution channels, you need to know when you will accomplish this in order to know when to start working on a secondary goal of increasing teddy bear production. You don't want a situation where you end up with more toy stores taking your teddy bears, but no teddy bears to give. Oh the horror!

Now that you have an understanding of SMART goals, head over to the second part to start planning your very on SMART marketing goals!

SMART Marketing Goals Template

What is your overall marketing goal?

How would you best summarize your marketing needs?

When would you like to meet this goal by?

What is your current (following, website traffic, fans, etc)? How many leads are you generating p/month?

How many hours per week can you dedicate to your Social Media?

What is the biggest marketing challenge preventing you from reaching this goal?

Social Media Strategies for Small Business

Any interaction through web-based or mobile devices which creates a dialogue between two or more people is considered social media. The key to *quality* social media though, is that it provides a medium to display user-generated content and encourages interaction. In plain English? Quality = Engagement.

These social networks allow for communications, typically referred to as "posts", from individuals. It is all user generated, so the members decide what will be seen and what will not. Each application and site has its own display of, and variation on, the definition of what a post is. Still, they are all very similar. Posts can be videos, images, links, or simply just words. The key: *It is content posted for others to view, review, and critique.*

The Major Platforms: Where You *Should* Be

Facebook

According to Statistica, there are 1.59 billion monthly users on Facebook. Largely image/video/text based, posts show as users' status or on others' "walls".This can act as a very successful feedback tool and it is a great for local businesses. It has more of an open forum format. With the introduction of new layouts, branding will become more prominent.

Facebook Strategies

Facebook has become a favorite destination for people, businesses, and organizations to connect and share information because of its easy to use and interactive features.

It's the most multimedia-friendly of the big three networks as members can post text, pictures, audio, and video, and can share their location too. It also offers tons of applications and widgets that can make your Facebook Page engaging and fun.

In a nutshell, Facebook works like this: Users sign up for a free account and then make connections with other users on the service by "Friending" them: When you find someone you know on Facebook, you request to be their "Friend." If the request is accepted, you can see that person's profile information, status updates, photos, and more.

Users who you accept as a Friend can, in turn, see your profile, status updates, and photos. If you don't want to share all your information with the public or all your Friends (for example, if you connect with coworkers or family members), there are privacy settings available to limit who can see what information you post or is posted about you by others.

Facebook is a great place to connect with your own friends, family, and colleagues, but it has also become an incredibly powerful platform for businesses and organizations to build community, engage with prospects, and encourage customers and members to spread your message to a larger network. Small businesses and nonprofits are encouraged to create a Facebook Page rather than personal profile.

A **Facebook Page**, like a personal profile, provides an information hub that users can choose to "Like." Liking a Facebook Page is not too different from subscribing to a newsletter. Facebook users will Like a Page to stay updated on events, promotions, and news, or to simply show their appreciation or endorsement. Anyone can build a Page —businesses, associations, actors, musicians, nonprofit organizations, politicians, etc.

A big advantage to creating a Facebook Page is that you do not have to accept requests for connections. When someone likes your Page, anything you do post to your Facebook Page will show up in their newsfeed. This is how the network effect kicks in. If you post something that your fans like, they will share it with their friends who may very well decide to connect with you too.

Finally, Facebook Pages are public, meaning they can get picked up in search engines and give you and your organization and its website, even more exposure.

What's also good about Facebook?

• The user base is huge, and that means many of your customers and constituents are already there.

• It's easy to use.

• You can post any type of multimedia content, including videos, photos, and links to external content.

• You can separate your personal and professional use.

Tips for Success:

People who connect with you or Like your Page are interested in what you have to say and appreciate what you do for them. Use that to your advantage by posting exclusive updates, photos, sales/promotions, and other content that will help to form an even closer bond with your customers and members.

When you post interesting content or exclusive promotions, your fans will Share or Like your message with their Friends. This can create an incredible network effect to drive more followers, email subscribers, and ultimately business.

Face Book Glossary

• Application (or App): A customizable, limited-used computer program that can be downloaded from a web page rather than being physically installed on a computer. Can be added to a Page, Profile, or Group to increase effectiveness and desirability by adding more features and functionalities.

• Blog (or Web log): An online journal/diary that is typically written by a single author. Can be made public or private. Blogs usually contain commentary on the author's personal life, favorite subjects, or current events. They may include multimedia elements such as pictures, videos, songs, or links to other websites. Can also be used as a verb, i.e., "Many Facebook members 'blog' about their daily lives to keep their friends informed."

• Chat: A Facebook feature that allows members to have real-time, text-based conversations with other members who are also logged in to Facebook.

• Fan: A Facebook member who has opted to be added to a database of other members who appreciate the contents of the page (or the person/product/company that it represents).

- Filter: A Facebook feature that allows members to search through their friends, photos, and other items by distinct, customizable categories.

- Friend: A Facebook member who has opted to be linked to another person's Profile, adding them to that person's social circle and giving them more in-depth access to that person's information. A "friend" invitation must be extended and accepted before information is shared. Can also be used as a verb, i.e., "If you 'friend' me on Facebook, I can share photos of my family with you."
You can also "unfriend" someone at any time. This action removes that person from your list of friends as well as your News Feed. Depending on your privacy settings, this action also limits a person's ability to communicate or share information with you.

- Group: A Facebook page that serves as a central online gathering place for Facebook members who opt to join because they share similar interests or causes. These are different than Pages and Profiles.

- Inbox:Like other online email systems, this is the location within Facebook where members can read and respond to email sent to them from other members.

- Like: A feature that allows a Facebook member to publicly appreciate a comment, post, video, picture, or other multimedia item shared by other members. A "like" appears as a "thumbs-up" icon directly beneath the shared item.

- Member:A person who has opted to join and participate within a Facebook Group. The person's Profile is linked to the Facebook Group, giving them real-time updates on the Group's activity.

- News Feed: A customizable, personalized list of activities occurring within a Facebook member's social circle. This information is sequenced chronologically and updated in real-time, giving individual Facebook members an up-to-date summary of what their friends and Groups opt to share.

- Page: A Facebook site created by a representative or collective group (rather than an individual) to share information and communicate directly with fans. These are typically used by artists, musical groups, celebrities, businesses, and brands. Although Facebook members can post messages on the Page's Wall, only the official administrator can create or edit the information. A Page is not the same as a Profile.

- Post: To share information or a multimedia element within your social circle. Can also be used as a noun, i.e., "I am going to post photos from my trip to Facebook."

- Profile: A Facebook site created by an individual who opts to share information and multimedia elements (such as pictures and videos) and communicate with other Facebook members. These are created by individual people and display personal information (such as hometown, education, favorite activities, and contact information) that the member opts to share with others. A Profile is not the same as a Page.

- Share: This function allows a Facebook member to host something they have found online (i.e., news article, photograph, YouTube video, or even another Facebook member's post) on their personal Wall.

- Status: Brief, text-based updates that Facebook members can create and share. These typically are used to inform friends of current whereabouts, activities, or thoughts. Once posted, they will appear in the News Feed of the people within a member's social circle. However, customizable privacy settings can control who can view these updates.

- Tabs: Links to different sections of a Page or Profile that are accessible on the main page. These are located directly beneath the main Profile picture.

- Tag: A Facebook feature that allows members to publicly identify the names of other members included in or related to a multimedia element (such as a photo or video). These can also be used as links to an individual person's Profile.

- Unlike: A Facebook member can remove his or her "Like" indicator from a comment or post; this action is referred to as "unliking" something.

- Wall: The location where members post information or messages directly to an individual's Page or Profile. This information is public and viewable by all members of Facebook.

Twitter

Largely text based. Posts are in the form of less than 140 character "tweets".Commonly used for branding. Retweets and trends are the quickest ways to get something noticed. 58% of users follow brands to find discounts. 39% of users follow brands for contests. If you have a sale, event, contest, or any limited time special, this is the place to post it.

Twitter Strategies

Twitter is one of the fastest growing social networks, with over 320 million users sending over 65+ million tweets each day.

Twitter is a real-time information network that empowers its users to share and discover interesting content through status updates (or "tweets"). Twitter is often referred to as a microblogging service because it limits your status updates to 140 characters. But the brilliance is in its simplicity and brevity.

For businesses and organizations, Twitter is one of the quickest ways to get a message out to people who may be interested in your activities, ideas, products, services, or events. You can also use Twitter to get real-time feedback from customers, members, and event attendees.

Like Facebook posts, users can share your tweet with the simple click of a button. This is called a "retweet," and it is the feature that makes Twitter such a great word of mouth platform that can help your message reach an entirely new group of prospective customers. (Hint: You should pay attention to people who retweet your message as that is a good indication that they are listening to what you say, and may be one of your best influencers. Your influencers are like your best friends because they can help you attract new followers and prospects.)

Twitter is a public site, which means anyone can view your tweets. However, users can choose to "follow" you on Twitter to keep track of your tweets. The follower relationship is not two-way; you don't have to follow someone for them to follow you, and vice versa. However, when you follow someone on Twitter, you'll see his or her tweets in real time on your private Twitter feed, including updates from everyone else you follow. (If you follow many people, this can create a bit of "noise," especially if those people are heavy users of the site.)

While you can only send private "direct messages" to people who follow you, you do not need to follow a user to send a public message to them; just include the handle (@username) in your tweet and it will show up in that user's feed. This is called an "@reply" or "mention."

You may discover that customers are already talking about you on Twitter by indexing your name with the "@" symbol or the "#" symbol.

Twitter is a great way to get real-time feedback from your customers and to discover what people are saying about you, your competition, industry, or any keyword that is relevant to you. You can see what people are saying about any topic in real time using Twitter's search tools.

What's good about Twitter?

• The "Timeline" (or the Twitter feed) is public, which can help to give your business or organization greater exposure in web search results.

• The site is like a public forum, so it's easy to build a community of potential customers you don't personally know.

• Customers and members can "follow" you without you having to reciprocate.

• There is a quick way to share links to content to help spread your message to a wide audience.

• Users are very vocal, so if they are happy with your business or organization, they'll say so.

What's not so good about it?

• It's sometimes challenging to create a meaningful post in only 140 characters.

• Lots of "noise." With so many identical looking tweets, you have to be creative to make a single one stand out in the crowd.

• Spammers are increasingly targeting the service.

• Users are very vocal, so if they have a problem with something, they'll say so (which is really not a bad thing).

Twitter's greatest strength is its vast reach. The more engaging and relevant your content is — whether it's an article you're sharing, a link to your newsletter, or words of support for the local lacrosse team — the greater the chances it will be passed on and retweeted to a whole new audience.

Twitter Glossary

• Activity: Lives in the "Connect" tab. Activity is a real-time dashboard to view what the people you're following are up to on Twitter. You can view Tweets they've favorited and discover other good content on Twitter.

• Algorithm: A computational procedure for solving a problem in a finite number of steps. Used frequently on Twitter to determine most popular Tweets and trends.

• API: An Application Programming Interface. Contains all Twitter data and is used to build applications that access Twitter much like our website does.

• Application (Third-Party): A third-party application is a product created by a company other than Twitter that's used to access Tweets and other Twitter data.

• Avatar: See Profile Picture.

• Bio: A short personal description of 160 characters or fewer used to define who you are on Twitter.

• Blocking: To block someone on Twitter means they will be unable to follow you or add you to their lists, and we will not deliver their mentions to your mentions tab.

• Bug: A bug is an internal error in our site code and functionality. We find and fix them all the time (nobody's perfect). If you see one, point it out to @support by sending a message.

• Buttons: Twitter buttons are available in the Resources tab of your account, and are used to link to Twitter from other webpages.

- Cache: A collection of stored data on your computer containing information that may be required in the future and can be accessed rapidly.

- Connect: The Connect tab lets you view interactions, mentions, recent follows and Retweets. Using the Connect tab you're able to view who has favorited or retweeted your Tweets, who has recently followed you, and all of your @replies and @mentions.

- Connections: The Applications tab in your Twitter settings shows all third-party websites and applications to which you've granted access your public Twitter profile. Revoke access at any time.

- Deactivation: A way to remove your profile from Twitter. Information from deactivated profiles remains in our system for 30 days.

- Developers: Engineers who don't work for Twitter, but who use Twitter's open-source API to build third-party applications.

- Direct Message: Also called a DM and most recently called simply a "message," these Tweets are private between the sender and recipient. Tweets sent over SMS become DMs when they begin with "d username" to specify who the message is for.

- Discover: The Discover tab is where you'd find top Tweets, Who to Follow, Activity, Find Friends, and Browse Categories. The Discover tab is all about, you guessed it, discovering new and engaging things to do on Twitter!

- DM: See Direct Message.

- Email Notifications: Preferences set by Twitter users to regulate notifications via email about events on your account, such as new followers and new direct messages.

- Favorite: To favorite a Tweet means to mark it as one of your favorites by clicking the yellow star next to the message. You can also favorite via SMS.

- FF: #FF stands for "Follow Friday." Twitter users often suggest who others should follow on Fridays by tweeting with the hashtag #FF.

- Follow: To follow someone on Twitter is to subscribe to their Tweets or updates on the site.

- Follow Count: The numbers that reflect how many people you follow, and how many people follow you. Found on your Twitter Profile.

- Follower: A follower is another Twitter user who has followed you.

- Following: Your following number reflects the quantity of other Twitter users you have chosen to follow on the site.

- Geolocation / Geotagging: The use of location data in Tweets to tell us where you are in real time. Is also called "Tweet With Your Location."

- GFF (Get Followers Fast): Sites that promise to get you more followers if you provide your username and password. After signing up, these sites send spam from your account. Don't use them.

- Hacked: See Hacking.

- Hacking: Gaining unauthorized access to an account via phishing, password guessing, or session stealing. Usually this is followed by unauthorized posts from the account. Users often use the word "hacking" for many things that are not hacking. Click here if you've been hacked. Read more about how to keep your account safe.

- Handle: A user's "Twitter handle" is the username they have selected and the accompanying URL, like so: http://twitter.com/username. Find out how to change your username.

- Hashtag: The # symbol is used to mark keywords or topics in a Tweet. It was created organically by Twitter users.

- Help Ticket: A request for help filed to our Support team via links in relevant articles on support.twitter.com. Also called simply a "ticket" or a "support ticket."

- Home: A real-time list of Tweets from those you follow. It appears on your Twitter home page.

- HT or h/t: Usually means "hat tip." A way of acknowledging the person who originally shared the content being tweeted, such as a link to an article or video.

- Impersonation: To pretend to be someone on the internet that you are not. Impersonation that is intended to deceive is prohibited under the Twitter Rules. Parody accounts are allowed.

- Interactions: A timeline in the Connect tab displaying all ways other users have interacted with your account, like adding you to a list, sending you a @reply, marking one of your Tweets as a Favorite, retweeting one of your Tweets.

- Known Issue: An error within our site that our engineers know about and are currently working to fix.

- Listed: To be included in another Twitter user's list. Listed numbers and details appear in the statistics section of your profile.

- Lists: Curated groups of other Twitter users. Used to tie specific individuals into a group on your Twitter account.

- Log In: The act of signing in to one's Twitter account on www.twitter.com or any third party application.

- Mention: Mentioning another user in your Tweet by including the @ sign followed directly by their username is called a "mention". Also refers to Tweets in which your username was included. Read more about replies and mentions.

- MMS: Multimedia Messaging Service (MMS), often called picture messaging, allows you to send media like audio or photos from your phone.

- Mobile Web: Twitter's website tailored to fit your mobile device. Visit it at mobile.twitter.com.

- MT: Similar to RT, an abbreviation for "Modified Tweet." Placed before the retweeted text when users manually retweet a message with modifications, for example shortening a Tweet.

- Name: A name that can be different from your username and is used to locate you on Twitter. Must be 20-characters or fewer.

- OAuth: A method to allow a user to grant a 3rd party access to their account without giving up their password.

- OH: "OH" most often means "overheard" in Tweets. Used as a way to quote funny things people overhear.

- Over Capacity Page: Users sometimes refer to this page as the "Fail Whale" page. The "Twitter is over capacity" message and a whale image shows up when our site is having trouble keeping up with traffic.

- Parody: To spoof or to make fun of something in jest. Twitter users are allowed to create parody Twitter accounts, as well as commentary and fan accounts.

- Phishing: Tricking a user to give up their username and password. This can happen by sending the user to fake login page, a page promising to get you more followers, or just simply asking for the username and password via a DM or email.

- Profile: A Twitter page displaying information about a user, as well as all the Tweets they have posted from their account.

- Profile Picture: The personal image uploaded to your Twitter profile in the Settings tab of your account.

- Promoted Tweets: Tweets that selected businesses have paid to promote at the top of search results on Twitter.

- Protected/Private Accounts: Twitter accounts are public by default. Choosing to protect your account means that your Tweets will only be seen by approved followers and will not appear in search.

- Query: A search performed to retrieve information from a database.

- Reply: A Tweet posted in reply to another user's message, usually posted by clicking the "reply" button next to their Tweet in your timeline. Always begins with @username.

- Reactivation: The act of bringing a deactivated account back to life on Twitter. It's alive!!

- Retweet (noun): A Tweet by another user, forwarded to you by someone you follow. Often used to spread news or share valuable findings on Twitter.

- Retweet (verb): To retweet, retweeting, retweeted. The act of forwarding another user's Tweet to all of your followers.

- RLRT: "Real Life Retweet" is another way of saying OH ("overheard"). Used to quote something a person said in "real life."

- Robot (Something's Not Working Error): An error message when something on our site is not working. (Hint: try refreshing the page to make him go away.)

- RSS Feed: Most commonly expanded as Really Simple Syndication. A family of web feed formats used to publish frequently updated works—such as blog entries or news headlines—in a standardized format.

- RT: Abbreviated version of "retweet." Placed before the retweeted text when users manually retweet a message. See also Retweet.

- Screencast: A digital recording (video) of a computer screen's output.

- Screenshot: An image captured on your computer or phone displaying your screen's output. Often used to share information with Twitter support agents while troubleshooting.

- Search (Integrated Search): A box on your Twitter homepage that allows you to search all public Tweets for keywords, usernames, hashtags, or subject. Searches can also be performed at search.twitter.com.

- Short Code: A five-digit phone number used to send and receive Tweets via text message.

- Sleep Time: Hours in which all mobile Twitter updates will cease to be delivered to your phone. Can be set up through your Settings tab.

- SMS: Short Message Service (SMS) is most commonly known as text messaging. Most messages are a maximum of 140 characters.

- Spam: Unwanted messaging or following on Twitter. We work hard to eliminate it.

- Suspended: The act of being prevented from using Twitter due to breach of our Terms of Service.

- Text Commands: When using Twitter via SMS, these commands allow you to access most Twitter features with simple text keywords.

- Third-Party Application: A third-party application is a product created by a company other than Twitter and used to access Tweets and other Twitter data.

- TIL: Acronym for "Today I learned." Often used at the beginning of a Tweet, for example: "TIL what a hashtag is!"

- Timeline: A real-time list of Tweets on Twitter. See also Home Timeline.

- Timestamp: A note displaying when a Tweet was posted to Twitter. Can be found in grey text directly below any Tweet. Is also a link to that Tweet's own URL.

- TL: Short for "Timeline." See also Timeline and Home Timeline.

- Top Tweets: Tweets determined by a Twitter algorithm to be the most popular or resonant on Twitter at any given time.

- Trends: A subject algorithmically determined to be one of the most popular on Twitter at the moment.

- Tweet (verb): Tweet, tweeting, tweeted. The act of posting a message, often called a "Tweet", on Twitter.

- Tweet (noun): A message posted via Twitter containing 140 characters or fewer.

- Tweet Button: A button anyone can add to their website. Clicking this button allows Twitter users to post a Tweet with a link to that site.

- Tweeter: An account holder on Twitter who posts and reads Tweets. Also known as Twitterers.

- Twitter: An information network made up of 140-character messages from all over the world.

- Twitterer: An account holder on Twitter who posts and reads Tweets. Also known as "Twitter user".

- Unfollow: To cease following another Twitter user. Their Tweets no longer show up in your home timeline. Learn how to unfollow.

- URL: A Uniform Resource Locator (URL) is a web address that points to a unique page on the internet. Find out how to shorten links.

- URL Shortener: URL shorteners are used to turn long URLs into shorter URLs. Shortening services can be found online. Find out how to shorten links. Learn about Twitter's own URL shortener.

- Username: Also known as a Twitter handle. Must be unique and contain fewer than 15 characters. Is used to identify you on Twitter for replies and mentions. Find out how to change your username.

- Verification: A process whereby a user's Twitter account is stamped to show that a legitimate source is authoring the account's Tweets. Sometimes used for accounts who experience identity confusion on Twitter.

- White-listed: A type of account that is allowed to go beyond the restrictions imposed by Twitter. This could be follower limits, posts, API access, etc. Learn more about whitelisting.

- Who to Follow: Who to Follow can be found in the Discover tab. Here, you should see a few recommendations of accounts we think you might find interesting. These are based on the types of accounts you're already following and who those people follow.

Instagram

Largely image based, video-sharing and social networking Posts are pictures and videos taken by its users, who can then apply digital filters to them, and share them on a variety of social networking services, such as Facebook, Twitter, Tumblr and Flickr. Currently, there are 400 million monthly active users on Instagram.

Instagram is a fast, beautiful and fun way to share your life with friends and family and of course, your clients.

It is an online photo-sharing, video-sharing and social networking service that enables its users to take pictures and videos, apply digital filters to them, and share them on a variety of social networking services, such as Facebook, Twitter, Tumblr and Flickr.[5] A distinctive feature is that it confines photos to a square shape, similar to Kodak Instamatic and Polaroid images, in contrast to the 16:9 aspect ratio now typically used by mobile device cameras. Users are also able to record and share short videos lasting for up to 15 seconds.

Instagram Strategies

Balance Fun Images With Pictures From Your Business

Rachel Sprung says, "Take advantage of the increased real estate you have with the Instagram web page to tell a story with the images. Have a healthy balance of fun images and business pictures."

Cultivate a Following

Tips for getting more followers on Instagram:

- Connect your Facebook account
- Use relevant, popular hashtags
- Engage by following others and liking their photos

Cross-post selected images to your Facebook page with a hashtag that aligns with your campaign or brand image to help people who don't know you're on Instagram to find you there.

Debut Videos

Video on Instagram has given Twitter's Vine a serious competitor to contend with. Most notably 15-second, filter-enabled, editable video functionality compared to Vine's 6.5 seconds. Instagram now allows videos to be up to 1 minute long.

Embed Instagram Video in Your Blog or Website

Instagram released an embed feature for its desktop web browser version. Since you never know who will see your shares on a social networking platform, embed your Instagram video in your blog or website to extend the reach of your content.

Follow Your Followers Back

The people you follow on social networking platforms make all the difference in the world. Curiously, many brands on Instagram (some with very large followings) don't follow back.

To create strategic relationships on Instagram, find the brands and people you enjoy and can learn from in your followers and follow them back.

Generate a Flexible Posting Plan

You don't need to post on Instagram every day. The 'feed speed' on Instagram is still mostly laid back. If you start posting a lot, you might saturate your followers' feeds, and you don't want to force yourself into the noise too often. Decide what you have ready to post and create a schedule to help you remember what to post when and to track what is working once you get going.

Inspire Potential Customers

Post photos that are relevant to your brand and potential customers: store events, sustainability and your active community of customers and employees.

Juxtapose Use of Filter Types and No-Filter Images

Instagram provides a number of filters to change the look and feel of your photos. A study conducted by Simply Measured earlier this year found 59% of the world's top brands are now active on Instagram.

Marketo also suggests that filters are more than a question of aesthetics, they can say a lot about you! Shake things up a little every now and then, and try out a new filter or go the no-filter route.

Kickstart Instagram Efforts With a Change in Perspective

For brands to be successful on Instagram, they need to get past their inherent interest in selling and instead:

- Share a distinctive view of the world
- Cultivate a unique visual sense
- Capture things that are interesting to the brand and to the core target customer
- Train your eye to focus on what makes a great, provocative, engaging image

Entrust your Instagram presence to someone in your business who understands how to align images with the interests of your target customer.

Market Your Brand Using Trends

Remember when Twitter's #followfriday seemed somewhat avant-garde? Instagrammers can use a number of trending hashtags to join in a bigger part of the visual community storytelling.

Use brand related hashtags and have fun: #ManCrushMonday or #SelfieSunday.

Network on Instagram

Instagram connects people through photos and suggests 3 essential ways to create a network:

- Engage—like others' photos and leave comments,

- Follow your already established followers from other social media platforms,

- Include your hashtags—if your brand uses specific hashtags on Twitter or Google+, use them on Instagram as well (Example: #ETTWomen, #5StepsToFabulous).

Optimize Your Profile

Instagram profiles—like their counterparts on Twitter, Facebook and other social networking platforms—need to include brand information in specific ways (e.g., maximum number of characters, specific image sizes, attention to branding).

Complete your profile with all of the information customers might need to find you and do business with you.

Promote Your Business on Both Facebook and Instagram

Great things can happen when a platform is purchased by an entity such as Facebook. Instagram and Facebook as a duo offer brands a unique opportunity for promotion.

Brands create Instagram videos, share them to their Facebook pages and then boost them into paid media that hits the Facebook news feed, in the same way that they boost text or photo posts. This enables brands to reach Facebook's 989 million monthly active mobile users, which dwarfs Instagram's 400 million. It's profiting from Instagram without having to advertise on Instagram… For now it's all about capturing and sharing moments—and paying to distribute them on the world's largest social network.

Capitalize on Facebook's integration of Instagram to reach a wider audience.

Quantify and Quality

Once you switch your IG profile to a business profile, you will be able to get important analytics about your Instagram account. You can also use image analytics tools such as BlitzMetrics and Curalate that will provide detailed insights.

Curalate is able to track an Instagram post's likes and comments so that a brand can see how that popularity translates into added followers, but also capitalize on the popularity. Use image analytics to identify images and video that resonate with your fans and followers.

Reward Followers

Offer your followers backstage entries to events, special offers, new products. Retail brands should reward their followers with discount codes and promos.

Showcase Photos of You and Your Team

Showing yourself , customers or team members at work not only gives a behind-the-scenes view of your company, it's also a way to celebrate your crew and show them how much they're valued.

Treat Followers to a Visual Experience

Sharpie shows followers how their product can be used to "start something" creative. The majority of their photos in their feed show drawings in a myriad of colors. Make sense? It should be interesting and fun!

Use Industry-Related Hashtags

If you're at an event or location that's designated by a hashtag (something like #360Academy), add it to your photos so that event coordinators and other attendees can find them.

Track the relevance of your Instagram hashtags with Nitrogram, the Instagram analytics and engagement platform that provides key metrics on hashtags including contributors, content, engagement and context.

Video Important Brand Moments

Brands can share unique branded experiences, highlight brand advocates, co-create content with audiences, preview products, highlight a specific cause, extend the brand's persona via video, preview upcoming events by adding visual context, share important news, drive promotional awareness, leverage Instagram video for promotion and create videos that show fan appreciation.

Capture your company's important moments in 15-second videos and share them with your followers so they feel included.

Widen Your Exposure to Other Brands

It's good practice to follow other brands on Instagram. Statigram is a great tool for finding brands and hashtags that relate to your brand. Simply enter the brand name or hashtag into the search box and click Search.

Use this tool to find, follow and research your competitors on Instagram.

Expose Something New

ABC World News often shares a photo about a broadcast they'll be doing later in the day.

Use Instagram to give your followers a first look at or sneak preview of an event, a product or new feature.

Yuck it Up

While running a business requires dedication, sweat and sometimes tears, it should never be all work and no play.

Instagram is perfect for displaying fun times in the office or when you're out and about having lunch or dinner with coworkers. Sharing these types of images with followers speaks volumes. It not only suggests that you don't take life too seriously while on the job, but instead you must be happy and successful in your career."

All work and no play will make your brand a dull company on Instagram. Integrate images that show your human side to create stronger connections with your followers.

Instagram Glossary

A 'post'
- A 'post' simply refers to an image uploaded to Instagram.
- A 'post' may include a caption, a geo tag and also tags of other users.

A 'like'
- Instagram (like many other social networks) is based on receiving likes, and liking other users' photos.
- You might 'like' an image by double tapping the image itself, or by clicking the 'like' button to the bottom left of the image.

Your 'username'
- Often referred to as your 'handle' your username is the name of your account – which people will type to find you, and which is also the address to view your profile online at www.instagram.com/[username] or www.ink361.com/[username]

A 'follower'
- Much like many other social media platforms, Instagram is based on 'followers.'

- A follower is a user who follow your account, and consequently sees every photo you publish on their feed.

A 'bio'

- The 'bio' section (the area below your 'name' on your profile) is an area designated to writing a small description about yourself, or about your brand.
- You can tell a lot from a 'bio' – too many emojis and phrases like 'shout outs 4 shout outs' or 'follow me!' might be warning signs for you though.

'Filters'

- The filter is perhaps Instagram's hallmark.
- Somewhat revolutionizing photo editing, before Instagram became the community platform for sharing and connecting it is now, many used the app to simply add *vintage style* effects to their personal photos.
- In short – there are 20 filters which are each a unique combination of different elements: including exposure, color balance, and contrast. Some filters also include frames, and can be added over a photo to the degree you choose. In fact, rather than using a filter at all – many people choose to manually edit their photos through Instagram's manual editing options instead.

The *hashtag*

- A word becomes an active 'hashtag' when it has the symbol '#' before it – and will appear in blue. *Check out the #ink361 hashtag for some cool photos!*
- The 'hashtag' has been one of the innovations brought by both Twitter and Instagram to social media; allowing users to connect with others, and discover images based on a common word or phrase.
- A hashtag can create a trends, and is often also used by marketers or event organizers to build a collection of images under a specific hashtag.
- If your posts are public, adding a hashtag to your photo allows your photo to be found by searching the hashtag, or by clicking on the hashtag once you have posted the comment.

A 'caption'

- Adding a caption to an image can be one of the most important aspects to contextualize, explain or capture someone scrolling through their feed.
- Unlike Twitter, the number of characters is far less limited.
- The caption is the breeding ground for the hashtag, and provides an opportunity to link photos to their relevant subject matters.
- To create paragraphs, users often create their captions under a word processor like the 'notes' app on an iPhone in order to format, and then copy this into the Instagram app.

Comments

- Simply, a user can comment on another users photo.
- However there is a key difference with *interaction* between Instagram, and say, Facebook. In order to receive a notification, you must be tagged by your 'username.' As a result, you will not simply receive a notification as a result of another user commenting on the same photo as you.

Your 'feed,' 'gallery' or 'album'

- Many refer to a user's collection of photos (posted to their profile) as their 'feed,' 'gallery' or even 'album.'

The 'posts' figure on a profile

- This is how many photos you, or another user, have posted in total.
- This may be an indication of how long someone has been using Instagram, or it may just show how frequently they post.

The 'News feed'

- Accessed by the 'home' button on the Instagram app, this shows a feed of the images from those you follow as they are uploaded, and so appears in chronological order.

Your personal 'activity' feed

- Your 'activity' tab will show you: when a user likes or comments on one of your photos; when a user mentions your username in a comment; when your photo is posted to the popular page and when you are tagged in a photo by another user.

The 'following' activity feed

- This shows a feed of photos that people you are following have liked or commented, and also accounts they have started following.
- This is normally limited to only showing around 5 minutes worth of information, after which no more history can be loaded.

The 'explore' tab

- This tab facilitates two important features: searching and discovering.
- Firstly, in terms of *discovering*: the explore tab defaults on the 'photos' category, displaying a collation of images (that were once solely the most popular photos on Instagram at that moment), curated as a selection of images from users similar to yourself or those suggested to you (based on who you already follow). This makes each users' 'explore' page unique. The other category of 'people' shows a similar list of people, in particular showing users from your other social networks, such as Facebook friends you are not yet following (and perhaps who's 10,000 cat photos don't require your attention!)
- The top of the explore tab also allows 'searching:' allowing you to search by hashtag or by user. This allows you to explore hashtags based on

relevant interests, events or themes; and searching by 'user' allows you to stalk or seek out any user on Instagram based on their username.

Suggested Users

- The team at Instagram select – based on an unknown but very much publicly debated criteria – a selection of users who become recommend as 'suggested users' to new users creating a profile.
- Suggested users are also followed by @Instagram for the period of which they are 'suggested.'
- Typically, users remain 'suggested' for around 2 weeks and can experience an influx of attention.

Private VS public

- Upon signing up, and indeed, even after, a user must choose between having a 'private' or 'public profile'.
- The essential difference is that public profiles can be viewed and followed by any user. Private profiles, on the other hand, require acceptance after a request is sent to follow.
- What you intend to use your profile for, and how you feel about privacy – will inform this choice. See more info on the Instagram privacy page!

Instagram 'direct'

- This feature allows you to send to a photo to single user, or a group – privately.
- This image doesn't appear on the news feed, search results or on any users' profile.
- The image you send can be edited in the same way as a post.

A 'Geotag'

- A 'geotag' is the location attached to an image, which corresponds to a longitude and latitude on a map.
- A list of local locations appear based on your position as determined by your device's location services. If not already existing, 'Geotags' can be created by a user.
- 'Geotags' allow your photos (If public) to be viewed alongside all other photos 'geotagged' at this location.
- 'Geotags' are a useful way to see images of the food at a café, the photos taken at an overseas fashion event, or even to collate a series of images geotagged at your own made *bed* (that is, for the days you just don't leave).

Pinterest

Largely image based. Posts are categorized. There are public comments on posts. Do you have a business with unique or new product ideas? Post them to Pinterest, and let its popularity carry the weight for you. This site is perfect for boutique or specialty stores. When posting, keep in mind, the American Pinterest population is over 60% female. The ratios are much more in most other countries.

Pinterest has captured our visual fancy like no other network before it.

The image-driven network's meteoric rise in only a few years shows the site is more than just a pretty community for people interested in fashion and lifestyle: Marketers are all over Pinterest's lead-generation aspects, and online hits on products from the site have proved a marketing sensation. According to a study by Shareaholic, the site drives more referral traffic than Google+, YouTube, and LinkedIn combined.

Pinterest Strategies

1. Set up a Pinterest Business account: You should consider opening up a business account on Pinterest. This isn't completely necessary, but it's definitely recommended if you plan to sell products via Pinterest. Similar to Facebook, a Pinterest business page will make your profile look more professional and more credible.

2. Use tools to help: There are tools for anything you might need:

- Try Piqora for a more complete Pinterest dashboard (including analytics and pin scheduling),

- Pinstamatic if you want your boards to be more fun and exciting,

- use Pinpuff if you want to calculate your influence, and

- check Repinly regularly to keep up to date with the most popular pins and boards.

If you are thinking of opening up your own Pinterest store to sell your products, take a look at Shopinterest – you'll be able to set up shop in a matter of minutes.

3. Check Pinterest Analytics regularly: In order to get the best results, you need to check your analytics regularly. Pinterest offers its own analytics. This allows

you to track how many people have been pinning from your website and how many people have viewed your pins. You can also get a glimpse into what's trending on Pinterest by checking the "most repinned" list. With this information you can then create better boards and start pinning more relevant pins to your target audience.

4. Make your website "pinnable": If you want people to start pinning from your website (which is an incredibly efficient way of spreading the word about your business) then you have to make your website and blog very visual. It can be challenging to find unique and "pinnable" images on a regular basis.

Many amateur and professional photographers license their work with the Creative Commons license, which means that you can use theses images so long as you provide credit and don't use the images for commercial purposes. The great part is that these images are often more interesting and exciting than regular stock photos, while also being free! Make sure that you always give credit where it's due.

Start by browsing these sites for sources of images:

• Flickr (be sure to check the copyright of images)
• Photo Pin (this site has a terrific selection of Creative Commons licensed images)

For paid royalty-free stock images, check out: Shutterstock, Flotilla, iStockPhoto

5. Know your audience: As with all other social networks, if you want to raise your engagement you have to do some research in order to understand your audience. You'll get a feel for what your audience likes to pin and what types of boards they are most interested in. With that information you will then be able to create better boards that your audience will want to follow and share with their friends and followers.

6. Pin to win! Contests are great promotional tools and Pinterest offers the perfect medium for running a contest. If you're just starting out on Pinterest and you want to get some likes and followers quickly, then running a contest might be the perfect solution. There are many apps that you can use to run a contest; some of my favorites include Woobox and Votigo. Make sure you read Pinterest's Terms of Service first so your contest doesn't end before it's time.

7. Engage: If you want people to engage with you, then you have to spend some time engaging as well. By regularly liking, commenting and pinning, you stand a much better chance to get more likes and comments from others as well as more followers. Make sure you stay true to your brand and pin only what you feel represents your business well.

8. Create infographics: Infographics are a great way of raising engagement and follower numbers on Pinterest. Among all your pins and repins, some original content–especially educational content–will give you an extra edge. And since Pinterest is mostly visual and image-based, infographics are the perfect solution. You'll find plenty great online tools to easily create infographics such as visual.ly or infogr.am.

Pinterest Glossary

- Pin: Pinterest helps people organize the things they love through the use of pins. A pin can consist of an image or video of a gift, recipe, destination, or quote. In order to populate your brand's Pinterest profile, your team will need to collect and pin individual pins to boards on your brand's profile.

- Board: Your brand's Pinterest profile is made up of boards, with pins on each board. A board is an opportunity for your brand to showcase various themes/interests/passions of your brand. You can create as many boards as you like, but you want to make sure that each board has a purpose and strategy behind it. Pinterest users can follow individual boards, or entire Pinterest profiles.

- Pinning: In order to turn a piece of content into a pin on Pinterest, a Pinterest user needs to take the first act of pinning the item. In order to pin a piece of content your brand owns, you can click on "upload a pin" to pin an image or video that lives offline, and "add from a website" to pin an image from online.

- Follower: A follower is any Pinterest user who has chosen to "follow" your brand. Once a user has become your follower, each pin/repin made by your brand appears in that user's Pinterest newsfeed.

- Following: If you follow a brand or a Pinterest user, you are their follower. Once your brand becomes a follower of a brand on Pinterest or a Pinterest user, anytime that user or brand makes a pin or a repin, it will show up in your newsfeed.

- Repin: Once a pin exists on Pinterest, users are free to repin that pin. Each time one of your brand's pins gets repinned, that pin will show up in the newsfeeds of all of the Pinterest users following the user who repinned your pin

- Newsfeed: There are three newsfeeds on Pinterest: your brand's newsfeed, another Pinterest user's newsfeed, and the Pinterest category newsfeed. The newsfeeds are the most active locations for content discovery on Pinterest. The most engaged pins across Pinterest within a given category show up in the categorical newsfeeds.

- Like: Similar to Facebook, Pinterest users are able to like pins. The difference between liking a pin and repinning it is that with liking, the user is not prompted to pin that pin to their profile and it does not show up in the newsfeed of their followers.

- Comment: Below the content of each pin is an open text box where users can make "comments." Although comments are not used too often by Pinterest users, there are some interesting ways to weave comments into a Pinterest contest execution. That being said, similar to a "like," a comment does not push that pin into the commenter's follower's newsfeeds.

LinkedIn

Largely text based. Posts are business oriented, and generally in the form of updates. Hands down, this is the best 'tried and true' method for business to business communications. With almost 2.5 million different businesses on LinkedIn, you have a vast opportunity to network with companies that could help you.

LinkedIn is the most "professional" social network of the Big Three and is most popular with business-to-business users and those looking for jobs. Individual users' profiles are tantamount to an online resume (complete with recommendations and endorsements) and, like Facebook, connections between users must be confirmed by both parties. Businesses and organizations can create profile pages that outline the who, what, and where of their operations, and in fact, many businesses use it to recruit (and check references) for new hires.

Two of the biggest benefits of LinkedIn are the community ("Groups") and question areas, which tend to be more professional in nature than those found on Facebook or Twitter. (It's one reason why LinkedIn is most popular with a business-to-business audience, rather than a business-to-consumer audience.) Answering questions in your area of expertise is a great way to establish you and your business or organization as an expert. LinkedIn is highly recommended for promoting a business-to-business event or communication since it is a professionally-oriented network.

What's good about LinkedIn?

• The "six degrees" nature of the site allows you to reach out to new people through your existing connections.
• Profiles are straightforward and connections are easy to make.
• It's a place where requests for endorsement are both welcome and expected.
• Allows for Question and Answer inquiries with a professional slant.
• It's a great place to look up background information on people before a meeting or phone call.

What's not so good about it?

• It's the smallest of the Big Three social networks, though its user base (more than 70 million users) is growing and active.
• Job seekers tend to be more active on the site than those already employed.
• People use the site for purely professional purposes, so marketing messages are not always welcome.

Participants in LinkedIn's Group forums are an active bunch who are looking for information and insight. Find the groups and discussion threads that are most relevant to your line of business or organization and add your expertise to the mix.

LinkedIn Glossary

• Connection: The people you invite or invite you. When you "accept" to form a connection with someone you form a first level relationship with them in your LinkedIn network.
• Degrees: A second degree connection means it is a friend of a friend, you are separated by two degrees. Three degrees away is someone you can read through a friend of a friend and one of their connections.

- Inbox: This is where you can check personal messages sent to you by other LinkedIn members.
- Introduction: Introductions are requests made to other LinkedIn members that you do not have a direct connection with. It is as it sounds, a way to introduce yourself to someone you do not necessarily know. LinkedIn limits the number of introductions you can have pending at one time.
- Invitation: This is what you send when you ask someone to connect with you. You invite them to join your network.
- Groups: Groups are exactly as they sound. They are groups of other LinkedIn users. Groups can be used as discussions or forums for people to connect or get advice and job postings.
- Network: Your network is the group of your connections, you are the center of your network. It can also include the connections of your connections.
- Profile: This is the page you control. It holds your picture and credentials. You have the ability to post job history and upload a resume. This is what others see when they click on your link.
- Recommendation: This is a request you can send out to have another LinkedIn member. If they agree, they will then write a short paragraph recommending you. This is visible to anyone who views your profile.

YouTube

Largely video based. Posts are videos and a description. There are public posts, or comments, under all videos. This is the king of viral marketing. If you don't have videos to upload yourself, it is really only useful as a buffer for your other social media efforts. However, if you do have videos to upload, by all means use it.

Youtube is one is popular for service industries and industries with complex products.

YouTube Strategies

1. Start by using the tools available directly through YouTube. For example, provide a detailed and accurate title and description to each of your videos, and associate tags (keywords) that are directly relevant.
2. Use a call to action within your videos to encourage people to like, rate, comment on and share your videos.

3. Begin by promoting your videos to the people you know, including your real-life friends, relatives, customers and clients. Ask these people to watch your video(s) and share them with their online friends.

4. Take advantage of the power and capabilities of the online social networking sites to promote your videos. As a spokesperson for your company, for example, become active on Facebook, Google+ and Twitter, as well as other relevant services. Be sure to create an online presence for your business on Facebook and/or Google+, and then use that presence to promote your videos.

5. Incorporate your videos into your own company's website and blog.

6. Share links to your videos with your existing customers or clients via opt-in email.

7. Use public relations techniques, such as using press releases to contact bloggers, editors, reporters and producers in order to generate free media coverage for your videos in mainstream media, as well as in blogs that cater to your target audience.

8. Get your videos (and your YouTube Channel page) listed with the major search engines, including Google, Yahoo! and Bing, and then focus on SEO strategies to get the best possible listing placements.

9. Try to collaborate on videos with other companies that are already utilizing YouTube effectively and that are targeting the same audience, but that are not in direct competition with you. This will allow you to capture the attention of your collaborator's viewers and subscribers.

10. Start promoting your YouTube channel within your company's printed catalogs, brochures, and sales materials, as well as within its existing traditional advertising.

11. Consider paying for keyword advertising on Google, Yahoo!, Bing and Facebook. Google AdWords for Video is also a very cost-effective and powerful tool for promoting YouTube videos.
12. If you have the budget, hire a YouTube video marketing company to help you plan and implement an online promotional campaign for your videos.

You Tube Glossary

- Annotations: Video Annotations are an uploader-controlled, dynamic overlay on videos that allows you to overlay text on a video and/or make parts of the video clickable. You can add, edit and delete annotations to your videos, controlling the text, placement, timing and link URLs. URLs can only be directed to YouTube.com.

- Audience Retention: The Audience Retention report (formerly known as Hot Spots in Insight) measures your video's ability to retain its audience. It shows when viewers fast-forward, rewind or leave your video.

- Avatar: The square image on your channel page that represents your channel across the site.

- Blog Outreach: A strategy of sharing your videos with a targeted list of blogs, sites and/or online communities and influencers. This includes sending your video link and/or embed code to blog editors and others in the hopes that they embed or share the video with their audiences.

- Blog Roll: A list of blogs, sites, online communities and influencers relevant to a particular category or type of content. Used for blog outreach.

- Bulletin: A message that channel owners can send to their subscribers. Bulletins show up in subscribers' feeds. Channel owners can attach videos to a bulletin.

- Calls to Action: (CTAs) These prompt the viewer to take an action.

- Channel or Channel Page YouTube.com/CHANNELNAME: A channel is the public page for a user account on YouTube. It contains uploaded videos, playlists, liked videos, favorited videos, channel comments and general activity. Some creators manage or create content across multiple channels.

- Comments These are written comments on videos, channels, playlists or in response to other comments. Comments may be posted either on the watch page or on a channel page.

- Community Actions Any actions taken by a viewer on or around your channel and content. Includes likes, favorites, subscriptions and comments.

- End-card or End-slate A graphic that creators include at the end of their videos. End-cards typically include specific Calls to Action to subscribe, watch more content, or visit a channel page. They may also contain credits for the video. Generally, end-cards prominently feature annotations.

- Engagement Interaction between the creator and the audience, the viewer and the video, or the creator and the site. Can be measured by the number of interactions (comments, favorites, likes, or new subscriptions) per view.

- Favorite(s) A user action that adds a video to their channel's Favorites playlist. This action can also be broadcast to subscribers

- Feed A stream of activity either for one channel (via the channel page feed) or for multiple channels (the homepage feed). Feed activities include uploads, updated playlists, video comments, channel comments, new subscriptions, bulletins, likes, favorites and sharing. Users control what feed activities they broadcast and, by subscribing to channels, what feed activities are broadcasted to them in their homepage feed.

- Hangouts on Air Google+ Hangouts are a live video chatting feature, and they can be broadcast on your YouTube channel.

- Hook Content that is meant to keep viewers interested in what happens next. Ideally, a video's hook happens within the first 15 seconds.

- Hosted Playlist A collection of videos linked by additional hosted videos. Hosted videos can act as intros, outros and/or interstitials. Hosted videos can contain an actual host (person) or creative branding that acts as a host.

- Like(s) A user action that shows appreciation for a video. This action can be broadcast to subscribers in the feed.

- Metadata The textual information that describes a video, channel or playlist. Video metadata includes title, tags and description. Playlist metadata includes title and description. Channel metadata includes a description.

- Optimization An action that increases the potential success of a video, channel, playlist or content strategy.

- Other Channels Module An optional module that allows the channel owner to feature other channels on their channel page.

- Packaging Graphics and/or content that adds context to a video. Packaging can build your brand, connect your host with the audience, add relevant context to archived content, or add scripted/annotated Calls to Action.

- Playlist A playlist is a collection of videos that can be viewed, shared and embedded like an individual video. You can create playlists using any videos on YouTube. Videos can be in multiple playlists. Uploaded videos and favorited videos are default playlists on your channel.

- Pre-buzz Audience interest in a tent-pole event occurring in the days and weeks leading up to it.

- Programming The practice and strategy of organizing videos, shows or channel content and activity into a daily, weekly or season-long schedule.

- Recommendation Activity A strategy in which a channel likes, favorites or comments on a video in order to promote that video to their subscribers through the feed.

- Series Playlist A playlist that locks the videos into one specific playlist. Meant for serial or episodic content that follows a narrative story arc, videos included in a series playlist cannot be added to other playlists on the channel.

- Share Ability to distribute videos via social media, email or direct links. This action can be broadcast to subscribers.

- Suggested Videos Video thumbnails that appear in the right-hand column of watch pages and the homepage, or the tiled thumbnails that appear when a video has finished playing.

- Subscriber / Subscription By subscribing to a channel, users will see that channel's activity in their homepage feed. Subscribers can also opt into email communication from subscribed channels on a per-upload and weekly digest basis.

- Subscriber Box See Other Channels Module.

- Tags Words or phrases used to describe the content of your videos. Added to videos at time of upload (see Metadata).

- Teaser A short video that acts as a preview or trailer for longer content. Can be used to promote larger content initiatives or announcements.

- Templates Different pre-set channel designs that can be used to highlight videos, playlists and other channels.

- Tent-pole Programming and Publishing Content creation and publishing strategy that is meant to draft off of the popularity of large cultural events. Programming and publishing tent-pole content is meant to maximize audience.

- Thumbnails The images selected to represent your videos or playlists on the site.

- Traffic Source The referral source of a video view. The page, module or site that drove a viewer to a video.

- Vlog A video-blog. A casual, conversational video format or genre featuring a person talking directly to camera.

- Watch Page The page where the majority of video viewing happens. URLs with the format youtube.com/watch?v=[video ID Here] are watch pages.

- Watch-time The amount of time in aggregate that your viewers are watching your videos. Watch-time is estimated in Analytics.

- YouTube Analytics A tool that provides information across various metrics for videos, channels and audience. Available in your user account.

Email Marketing

Email connects you to people. It's also where consumers spend the most money. When planning your email campaign, it's important to have a clear business objective.

Email Marketing Strategies

1. Personalize your email without using the recipient's name. No more "Dear [INSERT NAME HERE]".

The practice of personalized email greetings is not nearly as effective as it may seem. In fact, research by Temple's Fox School of Business suggests that **this particular kind of personalization could be harmful.**

Given the high level of cyber security concerns about phishing, identity theft, and credit card fraud, many consumers would be wary of emails, particularly those with personal greetings.

A significant element of email marketing is relationship. Does a recipient trust you? Does a recipient even know who you are? When an email jumps the gun by forcing familiarity too soon, the personalization comes across as skeevy. Intimacy is earned in real life, and it would appear to be the same way with email.

2. The long and short of subject lines.
When it comes to deciding how to craft that perfect subject line, there appears to be really only one area to avoid: the subject line of 60 to 70 characters. Marketers refer to this as the "dead zone" of subject length.

According to **research by Adestra**, which tracked over 900 million emails for its report, there is no increase in either open rate or clickthroughs at this 60-to-70 character length of subject line.
Conversely, subject lines 70 characters and up tested to be most beneficial to engage readers in clicking through to the content, and subject lines 49 characters and below tested well with open rate.
In fact, Adestra found that **subject lines fewer than 10 characters long had an open rate of 58%.**

Short subjects came in vogue with the success of President Barack Obama's email fundraising. He saw incredible engagement with subjects like "Hey" and "Wow."

So the question becomes: Do you want to boost clicks (response) or opens (awareness)? Go long for clickthroughs; keep it short for opens.

Either way, a helpful email strategy is to squeeze out more words or cut back just a bit to avoid that 60 to 70 character dead zone.

Subject Line Formula to keep in mind:

VERB + PURPOSE + OUTCOME

3. Morning between 9–11 a.m. is the best time to send email according to Campaign Monitor's 2016 research. It looks like there is a peak at 10 a.m. In short, 53% of emails are opened during the workday between 9 a.m.–5 p.m.

While many a quality email may be built during business hours, the ones with the best open rates aren't being sent from 9 to 5. The top email strategy is to send at night.

In their quarterly email report for 2012's fourth quarter, Experian Marketing Services found that the time of day that received the best open rate was 8:00 p.m. to midnight. This block not only performed better for open rate (a respectable 22 percent) but also for clickthrough and sales.
Inbox crowding and the deployment times of other marketers go hand-in-hand; if your email goes out when few others do, it stands a greater chance of getting noticed (so quick, start sending between 8:00 and midnight before everyone else catches on).

Optimal mailing for your customers' needs will be up to you. Test, test, and test some more to find out how your customer ticks and when he/she opens email.

4. The best content is free content: Give something away.

Consumers love a free lunch—or a free template (Visit *VCoppes.com/Resources* for some of my complimentary stuff).

In a study on their email list of 6,300 subscribers, Bluewire Media tested various types of content to see what led to the highest rates for opens and clicks. The winner was templates and tools, just the kind of freebies that email readers want

Many a consumer will ask, "What's in it for me?" When it comes to resources, Bluewire Media's test results say that templates and tools outweigh ebooks, expert interviews, brain teasers, and even photo albums. You will want to test with your own list, but certainly use Bluewire's research as a head start.

5. Mobile opens accounts for 66 percent of all email opens.

Mobile opens accounted for 68% of all email opens in June, according to numbers provided by Marketing Land. If your email list accounts for $100,000 in sales each month, could you afford to wave bye-bye to $68,000 just because your email looks funky on a mobile phone?

Design responsively to ensure that your email looks great no matter where it's read. Here are some quick mobile design tips:

- Convert your email to a one column template for an easy mobile fix.
- Bump up the font size for improved readability on smart phones.
- Follow the iOS guideline of buttons at least 44 pixels wide by 44 pixels tall.
- Make the call-to-action obvious and easy to tap. Above the fold is preferable.
- Consider ergonomics. Many users tap and scroll with their thumb, so keep important tappable elements in the middle of the screen.

6. Email still reigns over Facebook and Twitter.

Social media may be the young whippersnapper nipping at email's heels, but the content king of the inbox still holds sway in social influence, according to a study by SocialTwist. Over an 18-month period, SocialTwist monitored 119 referral campaigns from leading brands and companies. The results showed a significant advantage to email's ability to convert new customers compared to Facebook and Twitter.

Of the 300,000 referrals who became new customers, 50.8 percent were reached by email, compared to 26.8 percent for Twitter and 22 percent for Facebook.

7. Send email on the weekends.

While not as overwhelming a winner as the 9 to 5 time of day, Saturday and Sunday did outperform their weekday counterparts in Experian's study of day-of-week performance.

8. Re-engage an inactive group of subscribers

Your list is huge. Great! The only problem is that two-thirds of it may be inactive.

Research has found that the average inactivity for a list is 63 percent, meaning that once someone joins they are less likely to ever follow-up with your follow-up emails. Email marketing firm Listrak goes so far as to identify the first 90 days as the window for turning a sign-up into a devotee (and they lay out a plan for doing so).

What's to become of that inactive 63 percent? Re-engagement campaigns are an excellent place to start.

Email Marketing Glossary

- Above-the-fold - The part of a web page that is visible without scrolling. It is generally more desirable placement on a Website because of its visibility. If you have a "join our mailing list" tag on your Website, you should place it "above the fold" making it easy for visitors to opt-in.
- CPM (Cost per thousand) - In email marketing, CPM commonly refers to the cost per 1000 names on a given rental list. For example, a rental list priced at $250 CPM would mean that the list owner charges $.25 per email address.
- CTR (or Click-through rate) - The percentage (the number of unique clicks divided by the number that were opened) of recipients that click on a given URL in your email.
- Conversion rate - The number or percentage of recipients who respond to your call-to-action in a given email marketing campaign or promotion. This is the measure of your email campaign's success. You may measure conversion in sales, phone calls, appointments etc.
- Email blacklist - It is common for an ISP to a use a blacklist to determine which emails should be blocked (see "email blocking"). Blacklists contain lists of domains or IP addresses of known and suspected spammers. Unfortunately, these blacklists also contain many legitimate email service providers. Just a few spam complaints can land an email service provider or IP address on a blacklist

despite the fact that the ratio of complaints to volume of email sent is extremely low.

- Email blocking - Email blocking typically refers to blocking by ISPs or corporate servers. Email blocking occurs when the receiving email server (e.g. Yahoo!, AOL, Hotmail etc) prevents an inbound email from reaching the inbox of the intended recipient. Most of the time the sender of the email receives a "bounce" message notifying the sender that their email has been blocked. ISPs actively block email coming from suspected spammers.

- Email filters – "Filtering" is a technique used to block email based on the content in the "from:" line, "subject:" line, or body copy of an email. Filtering software searches for key words and other indicators that identify the email as potential spam. This type of blocking occurs on a per email basis.

- Email newsletter ads or sponsorships - Buying ad space in an email newsletter or sponsoring a specific article or series of articles. Advertisers pay to have their ad (text, HTML or both depending on the publication) inserted into the body of the email. Email newsletter ads and sponsorships allow advertisers to reach a targeted audience driving traffic to a website, store or office, signups to a newsletter or sales of a product or service.

- Email whitelist - A whitelist is the opposite of a blacklist. Instead of listing IP addresses to block, a whitelist includes IP addresses that have been approved to deliver email despite blocking measures. It is common practice for ISPs to maintain both a blacklist and a whitelist. When email service providers, like Constant Contact, say they are "whitelisted" it means that their IP addresses are on a specific ISP's whitelist and are confident that emails sent using their service will be delivered.

- False positive - A false positive occurs when a legitimate permission- based email is incorrectly filtered or blocked as spam.

- Hard bounce/Soft bounce - A hard bounce is the failed delivery of an email due to a permanent reason like a non-existent address. A soft bounce is the failed delivery of an email due to a temporary issue, like a full mailbox or an unavailable server.

- House list (or Retention list) - A permission-based list that you built yourself. Use it to market, cross sell and up-sell, and to establish a relationship with customers over time. It is one of your most valuable assets because it is 7 times less expensive to market to an existing customer than it is to acquire a new one. Use every opportunity to add to it and use it.

- HTML email - Sending HTML email makes it possible to include unique fonts, graphics and background colors. HTML makes an email more interesting and when used properly can generate response rates up to 35% higher than plain text.

- Open rate - The percentage of emails opened in any given email marketing campaign, or the percentage opened of the total number of emails sent.
- Opt-in (or Subscribe) - To opt-in or subscribe to an email list is to choose to receive email communications by supplying your email address to a particular company, website or individual thereby giving them permission to email you. The subscriber can often indicate areas of personal interest (e.g. mountain biking) and/or indicate what types of emails they wish to receive from the sender (e.g. newsletters).
- Single Opt-In (with a subscriber acknowledgement email) - The most widely accepted and routinely used method of obtaining email addresses and permission. A single opt-in list is created by inviting visitors and customers to subscribe to your email list. When you use a sign-up tag on your website, a message immediately goes out to the subscriber acknowledging the subscription. This message should reiterate what the subscriber has signed up for, and provide an immediate way for the subscriber to edit interests or opt-out.
- Confirmed Opt-In (a.k.a. Double Opt-In) - A more stringent method of obtaining permission to send email campaigns. Confirmed opt-in adds an additional step to the opt-in process. It requires the subscriber to respond to a confirmation email, either by clicking on a confirmation link, or by replying to the email to confirm their subscription. Only those subscribers who take this additional step are added to your list.
- Opt-out (or Unsubscribe) - To opt-out or unsubscribe from an email list is to choose not to receive communications from the sender by requesting the removal of your email address from their list.
- Permission-based email - Email sent to recipients who have opted-in or subscribed to receive email communications from a particular company, website or individual. Permission is an absolute prerequisite for legitimate and profitable email marketing.
- Personalization – Addressing individual recipients by first name, last name or both dynamically in an email. Personalization can also include a reference to previous purchases, or other content unique to each recipient. Avoid using personalization in the subject line of your emails as this is a tactic widely used by spammers.
- Privacy policy - A clear description of a website or company's policy on the use of information collected from and about website visitors and what they do, and do not do, with the data. Your privacy policy builds trust especially among those who opt-in to receive email from you or those who register on your site. If subscribers, prospects and customers know their information is safe with you,

they will likely share more information with you making your relationship that much more valuable.

- Rental list (or Acquisition list) - A list of prospects or a targeted group of recipients who have opted-in to receive information about certain subjects. Using permission-based rental lists, marketers can send email messages to audiences targeted by interest category, profession, demographic information and more. Renting a list usually costs between $.10 and $.40 per name. Be sure your rental list is a true permission-based, opt-in list. Permission-based lists are rented, not sold. Don't be fooled by a list offer that sounds too good to be true or by someone who tries to mislead you by calling their list "targeted" or "clean" without certifying that it is permission-based.

- Signature file (or sigfile for short) - A tagline or short block of text at the end of an email message that identifies the sender and provides additional information such as company name and contact information. Your signature file is a marketing opportunity. Use it to convey a benefit and include a call- to-action with a link.

- Spam or UCE (Unsolicited Commercial Email) - Email sent to someone who has not opted-in or given permission to the sender. Characteristically, spam is unwanted, unexpected email from a sender unknown to the recipient.

- Targeting - Selecting a target audience or group of individuals likely to be interested in a certain product or service. Targeting is very important for an email marketer because targeted and relevant email campaign, yield a higher response and result in fewer unsubscribes.

- URL (or Universal Resource Locator) - A website, page or any other document address or location on the Internet that indicates the location of every file on every computer accessible through the Internet.

- Viral Marketing - A type of marketing that is carried out voluntarily by a company's customers. It is often referred to as word-of-mouth advertising. Email has made this type of marketing very prevalent. Tools such as "send this page, article or website to a friend" encourage people to refer or recommend your newsletter, company, product, service or specific offer to others.

Blogging

Blogging is one of the most valuable tools that businesses have to engage with customers and ultimately serve them better.

BLOGS ARE MOST IMPORTANT FOR SEO AND SEO Is The Most Important Digital Marketing Tactic.

Building a client-based business is not easy. If you're spending hours every week on an activity that's not bringing you quality leads, you're making it harder on yourself than it has to be.

TRUTH: You're keeping yourself from making money by wasting the most valuable resource that you have: *your time.*

If you're not blogging, it's time to get started. Here are 4 ways to spend your blogging time more wisely and productively:

1. Solve one problem per post: High-paying clients tend to be busy so they're willing to pay more to get things done because because A) they don't have time to do everything themselves; and/or B) their time is worth a lot to them.
This means that they aren't browsing the Internet searching for interesting blog posts to read and if they've made it to *your* blog, they're probably looking for something specific.

So, give. them. what. they're. looking. for. Make it easy for them to find.
If you solve 1 problem per post, your readers will be able to do a quick search, find the post that is relevant and find the answer they need. And you my friend, you want to be the person they turn to when they need something. This way, when they need something bigger than a blog post, your name is the first one that will come to mind.

When your clients think of you, you want them to think of how quick, smart, helpful, knowledgeable and to the point you are.
Most importantly, you want your clients to see *how highly you value their time.* Treat their time like the precious gem they believe it to be, and you'll become a gem of a resource to them.

2. Speak your clients' language: Your client doesn't know as much as you do about your area of expertise, hence why they need you.
If you're talking about what they need in technical terms, you're missing an opportunity to connect with the people who need you. Instead, write in the terms your clients actually use. Yeah, like use actual colloquial, every day terms.

Say your ideal clients are local businesses who want to use the Internet to expand their clientele. How do they describe their needs?

- "I need to learn how to install WordPress."
- "I need to get a web designer, an SEO expert, and a social media consultant."
- "I need to figure out this whole Internet thing."

It could be any of these, of course. The key is to figure out how *your* ideal clients actually speak, so you can relate to them on their terms.

3. Tell your readers what to do next (and make it easy): Your client shows up at your blog. She/he reads your post, loves your work and thinks you're fabulous! Now what?

Are you telling your reader what to do next or are you just letting her/him wonder around, looking at all the things she *might* do:

- Go to your "Contact" page, fill out the form, and wait for you to call her back.
- Sign up for your e-mail list.
- Go to your "Services" page, find the relevant service, and pay for it using a Paypal button you conveniently placed at the bottom.
- Call the phone number on your "Contact" page.
- Set up a free consultation.
- Download a free resource.
- Check out your "links you love" page.
- Read other posts on your blog.
- Leave a comment on your blog.
- Subscribe to your RSS feed.
- Sign up for your free newsletter/webinar, etc.

How much time do you think your potential client will spend trying to figure this out?

Probably about as much time as you spent reading that list (which is not long). Become your prospects' guide instead of letting them stumble around.

At the end of every post, tell your reader exactly what to do next. Make it a simple, low-risk task that requires next to no thought.

For example:
Click here and enter your e-mail to learn more about how [your great service] can help you with [their problem].

Then follow up with some useful information about your services and an invitation to talk by phone for a few minutes. Keep it simple.

4. Stop writing about yourself (or stop blogging): Your blog shouldn't be about you. It should be about your clients.

I'll be the first one to tell you that what this means is that you can totally write about yourself but in a way that's relevant to your potential clients.
Telling a story that helps potential clients understand your commitment to quality? Good.

Telling a story that helps potential clients understand what a PITA your kids can be sometimes, or how your last selfie doesn't really capture your essence and that by the way you're thinking of eating raw? Not so good.

Sharing details of your personal life can help potential clients *know, like and trust you*. That can be very powerful.

Oversharing, however is not interesting to your clients. The thing that interests your potential clients is how you can help them, and what you would be like to work with. Give them what they want.

If you can't give potential clients what they want, stop blogging.

Bottom line, if you're spending several hours every week on a blog that doesn't interest your potential clients, you're not marketing. You're either wasting your time or writing what should be a personal blog.

If you're spending a lot of time trying to figure out what to write about, you should probably be blogging less and talking with your potential clients more. Seriously. Just talk to them.

Offer a free consultation, spend some time helping them with their current issue, and then ask a few questions. See what comes up.

Talking (and listening) to people in your target market is the best way to generate ideas for your blog. It's the best way to find out your potential client's problems, concerns, and the language they use to talk about those things.

Blogging Glossary

- Above the fold: A newspaper term that also refers to the top area of a website that can be seen when the page first loads, before scrolling down.
- A/B testing: Testing of an advertisement, sales page or piece of content conducted by creating alternate versions and seeing which one visitors respond to the best.
- Advertorial: A piece of content that is an advertisement, but written and
- designed to look like a regular post (editorial). See also: Sponsored post.
- Affiliate: A person who engages in affiliate marketing.
- Affiliate link: A URL that identifies an affiliate and tracks traffic sent to a merchant's website.
- Affiliate marketing: One way bloggers can monetize their site by using a special link to link to another website's products or services in return for a commission, usually a percentage of the sale price, if purchased within a specified period of time.
- Affiliate program: A program where a merchant (seller) rewards an affiliate for sending them traffic, sales or leads. May also be called a referral program, associate program or revenue-sharing program.
- Ajax: A technique that allows users to send and receive data without reloading the entire page.
- Akismet: A popular WordPress plugin designed to filter spam.
- Alexa: An analytics website often referred to when comparing websites against one another. Provides a ranking and information on traffic, audience demographics, and inbound links.
- Algorithm: The formula that determines how one of your blog's pages or posts ranks within a search engine's search results.
- Alt attribute: The alt attribute within HTML or XML documents specifies alternative text to be displayed should elements not render on a page correctly.
- Anchor text:The clickable text in a hyperlink. The choice of words used in anchor text is important for search engine optimization.
- API: Application Programming Interface. The set of programming instructions and rules by an application that allows other applications to communicate with it.
- App: Short for application. Optional software used on your computer or phone.
- Audience: The people who read your blog, follow your tweets, like your Facebook page etc.

- Automattic: The company behind popular blogging resources including the WordPress platform.
- Avatar:The graphical representation of yourself on a website. That is, the image you use to create a profile on forums, online accounts etc. See also: Gravatar.
- Backlinks: Links that point from one website to another.
- Backup Buddy: A popular WordPress plugin used to create full blog backups and restorations.
- Back end: The area of a website where authorized users can modify content, sometimes referred to as the administration area or panel. See also: Front end.
- Badge: A badge is a way for bloggers to encourage other bloggers to promote their blog by placing an image on their site that links back to the badge owner's blog. Usually 125 x 125 pixels in size. See also: Button.
- Bandwidth: The amount of traffic and data that is allowed to occur between your website and the internet.
- Banner: A banner can refer to a blog header. It is also sometimes used as another name for a blog add.
- Bing: The name of Microsoft's search engine.
- Bit.ly: A website that lets you shorten and track URLs.
- Blackhat SEO: Methods of improving a website's ranking in search engines that are considered wrong or deceptive.
- Blog: A type of website with content called posts that are often presented in reverse chronological order. Visitors can usually leave comments on posts.
- Blogger: A person who owns a blog. Also the name of a blogging platform owned by Google.
- Blogosphere: The blogging community.
- Blog roll: A collection of links on a blog, usually favorites as chosen by the blog's owner/s.
- Blogspot: The subdomain of blogs created using Google's Blogger platform.
- Bookmark: To save a URL for visiting later.
- Bookmarklet: Code (usually JavaScript) used to create a faux bookmark, that when clicked, performs a function such as the Pinterest "Pin It" bookmarklet.
- Bounce rate: The percentage of people who arrived on your site and only viewed one page before leaving.
- Browser: A program such as Google Chrome, Firefox and Safari, used to view pages on the internet.

- Button: See badge.
- Captcha: Letters and/or numbers you're sometimes required to enter before submitting a comment, password or other data on a website, designed to ensure the response is created by a human and not a computer.
- Carnival: A blogging event where bloggers create posts based on a theme or topic. Generally one blogger "hosts" the event, and participants submit links to show their participation.
- Category: A way of grouping blog posts into topics.
- Child theme: Within WordPress, a child theme is a theme that inherits the functions of a another theme (a parent theme), and allows you to modify it.
- Click-through rate: The number of times an add is clicked on, presented as a percentage of the number of impressions it receives.
- Cloaked links: Affiliate links that have been converted into a different-looking link (eg: yourblogname.com/recommends/shopname) for reasons including ease of listing or sharing, tracking clicks, or to simply make them look less like an affiliate link.
- CMS: Content Management System. Software that allows creation, publishing and management of a website's content. See platforms.
- Comments: The thoughts or feedback left by a blog's readers in relation to a blog post.
- Commission: Income an affiliate earns for generating a sale or lead for a merchant's products or services.
- Conversion rate: The percentage of visitors who convert visits or page views into some type of action, such as signing up for a newsletter, or purchasing an e-book.
- Contextual advertising: Advertisements that display on a website based on a visitor's search history, or words (keywords) that have been used on the website.
- Cookie: Small text files stored on your computer designed designed to save information on a user's computer for a blog or website to retrieve later (such as login details).
- cPanel: A web-hosting control panel that provides an interface and tools for the user to manage the hosting of their blog or website.
- CPC: Cost Per Click. The amount you may earn each time a visitor clicks on an ad displayed on your blog. The amount is determined by the advertiser.
- CPM: Cost Per Mille (mille = thousand). The amount you'll earn from an ad each time is displayed 1000 times on your blog.
- Creative Commons: A non-profit organization that released several copyright licenses designed to help the creators of works (photos, music tracks

etc) communicate which pieces are available for others to use, adapt or share.

- CSS: Cascading Style Sheets. Files that define how to display HTML elements. You'd edit a CSS file, for example, to make all of your post headlines a different color.
- CSS sprites: A collection of images or icons combined into one larger image called a sprite sheet. They are used to render performance and are displayed using CSS.
- CSV: Comma Separated Values. A type of file that stores plain-text data (such as newsletter subscriber information) made up of records and fields. Each field is separated by a comma or tab.
- Dashboard or dash:The "behind the scenes" admin area of your blog where posts are created, comments are moderated and so on.
- Deep linking: Creating posts with links pointing to numerous pages on your blog, excluding the homepage, with the purpose of driving traffic to various articles, thus encouraging visitors to stay on your blog longer.
- Div: A CSS term that divides content into containers so that each container can be formatted (styled) differently.
- DIY: Stands for Do It Yourself; a term used by many craft and decorating bloggers when creating tutorial-type posts.
- Domain name:A string of letters, numbers and/or hyphens, separated by periods, that you type into your browser to visit a particular website.
- Domain-name registrar: An accredited organization that handles the registration of domain names.
- Dooced: To lose one's job because of one's website. Coined by popular mommy blogger, Heather Armstrong of Dooce.com.
- E-book: A PDF document, sold or given away by bloggers either in return for money, or as a tool to encourage visitors to sign up for a blog's newsletter, liking a Facebook page or more.
- E-mail marketing: A form of direct marketing which uses email to communicate broadcast messages to its audience (also known as sending newsletters).
- Embed: To place content from another website within your own blog's post or page.
- Evergreen content: A type of post that does not date quickly, and is therefore as relevant today as it will be in years to come. For example: 25 Timeless Trends (as apposed to This Season's Top 5 Trends).
- Favicon: Also known as a favorite's icon, a favicon is the small symbol (usually adapted from a website's logo) that appears in browser tabs, book marks.

- Facebook: A social-networking website. Related list: Facebook tools.
- Flat design: A web design term that refers to a way of designing without adding three-dimensional attributes. See also: Skeuomorphism.
- Flickr: A photo-sharing and networking website that also provides creative commons content.
- Footer: The bottom area of your blog that usually contains a copyright notice as well as links to about and contact pages, terms of service, privacy policies and monetization disclosures.
- Forums: Discussion boards where users can connect, share thoughts, and/or seek support.
- Front end: The area of your blog that your visitors see when they visit your site. See also: Back end.
- FTC: Federal Trade Commission. A US department that aims to (amongst other things) prevent business practices deemed unfair.
- FTP: File Transfer Protocol. Used to upload website files from your computer to your server.
- Gravatar: A global avatar. Uses an image associated with an e-mail address to show the author's avatar (image) whenever they leave a comment with that address.

- Gallery: Collection of images displayed within a blog post. They either display when enlarged one-by-one, or as a click-through style slideshow.
- Ghost blogging: To write a blog post or manage a blog anonymously or under a different name.
- GIF: Graphics Interchange Format. A file type best used when saving logos or graphics with block colors. Supports transparency and animation.
- Geotargeting: A method of determining a blog visitor's whereabouts, and displaying content to them based on their location.
- Gmail: A free e-mail system created by Google.
- Google+: A social network created by Google.
- Google Adsense: A contextual advertising program created by Google.
- Google Analytics: A free and powerful analytics tool created by Google.
- Google Feedburner: A web-feed management tool provided by Google.
- Google Reader: A free RSS reader by Google.
- Gravity forms: A WordPress plugin designed to make creating and managing forms of all kinds easy and powerful.
- Hashtag: A method of tagging a post within networks such as Twitter or Instagram so that viewers can see all related updates or images by other users.

- Header: The top area of your blog that contains your blog's logo.

- Heat map: A map of your blog, showing which areas of a specified page are clicked on the most, usually represented using colors where one color indicates a high number of clicks while another represents a low number of clicks.
- HTML: Hyper Text Markup Language. A language that uses tags to describe the content of a website's page.
- Hotlinking: Using an image on your website that's being hosted on another website.
- htaccess: A file placed in the directory level of your website that allows for decentralized management of web server configuration.
- Hyperlink: A linked image or text on a website or digital document that, when clicked, takes you to another page on the internet.
- IAB: Interactive Advertising Bureau. Website dedicated to the growth of interactive advertising. Provides guidelines, standards and best practices.
- iFrame: A method of including one HTML page within another HTML page.
- Impression: A view of a single item, whether it's a page, or an ad, on your blog.
- Inbound link: A link on a blog or website that points to your blog or website.
- Indexed: A web page that has been found by a search engine and included within its search results.
- Instagram: A photo-sharing app and social network, popular for its photo filters.
- Internal link: An internal link is a link that points to another section or page of the same website.
- IP address: A unique string of numbers that identifies every computer that's connected to the internet.
- IRL: Stands for In Real Life.
- JavaScript: A programming language used to make websites interactive.
- JPG/JPEG: Joint Photographic Expert's Group. An image file format used to compress information within a photo or picture.
- Jump: Creating a "jump" means adding in a link so that your visitors see a summary of your blog post with a read-more link for them to click on should they wish to view the whole post.
- jQuery: A JavaScript library designed to make it much easier to use JavaScript on your website.
- Keywords: Words that users enter into search engines to find a relevant page or pages, these words can also be used by bloggers within their posts to get traffic via search.

- Keyword stuffing: The practice of using too many (and sometimes irrelevant) keywords in posts or the blog's HTML in an attempt to get traffic via search engines.
- Keyword research: The act of finding out which keywords search-engine users are searching for to find information.
- Klout: A website that aims to measure the influence of social-network users including those on Twitter.
- Landing page: A dedicated page on a website created with the intention of converting visitors into sales leads or e-mail marketing subscribers for a particular product or database list.
- Leader board: The name for a popular-sized website advertisement that's 728 pixels wide by 90 pixels high.
- Lightbox: The practice of showing images or files as an overlay on the current blog page (causing the rest of the page to be darkened) instead of causing a new page to load.
- Link bait: Website content created with the aim of gaining attention and inbound links.
- LinkedIn: Social-networking website for people interested in connecting with others for business opportunities.
- Live pinning: A way of creating engagement on Pinterest by pinning images (such as those from a runway show) in real time.
- Long-tail keywords: A keyword phrase made up of at least three to five words.
- Loop: In WordPress, the loop is the PHP code used to display posts.
- LOTD: Look Of The Day. A fashion blogger term for a daily outfit post.
- Lurker: Someone who regularly reads a blog but does not leave comments.
- Malware: Short for malicious software. Code or scripts designed to disrupt software or collect information such as passwords.
- Media kit: Document, slideshow or web page containing information about a blog's traffic, achievements, advertising rates, and sponsorship opportunities used when forming partnerships or selling ad opportunities.
- MedRec: Short for medium rectangle. The name for a popular-sized website advertisement that's 300 pixels wide by 250 pixels high.
- Meme: On the internet, a meme is a concept or idea (image, video etc) that spreads quickly. E.g.: the Sh*T Girls' Say-related videos.
- Merchant: A person selling goods or services.
- Micro blog: A blog with very short content. Twitter is considered a micro blog.
- Micro niche: A subset of a niche. For example, a blogger could target the beauty market with their content, but to specialize they could target the

niche market of make-up, and to go one step further they could target the mineral make-up market.

- Mobile site: A website or blog that's been optimized to be viewed on a mobile device such as a smart phone or tablet.
- Navigation: A collection of text or image links that form a blog's menu.
- Newsletters: An e-mail communication tool used by bloggers to alert their subscribers of updates, important news, downloads or more.
- Niche: A subset of a market. For example, a blogger could target the beauty market with their content, but to specialize they could target the niche market of make-up.
- Nofollow: The nofollow value is like a stop sign given to certain hyperlinks, instructing some search engines that the link should not influence the targeted site's ranking in search engine results. It's designed to help reduce spam, especially in blog comments.
- Notification bar: A bar that sits along the top or bottom of your blog, with the intention of sending a message of your choice to your visitors. For example: a link pointing to a free download you may be offering.
- Organic search results: Listings that appear on search engines results pages because their content is relevant to the searched word or phrase, unlike those results that appear due being paid advertisements.
- Outbound link: A link that points to an external website or web page.
- Outsourcing: Hiring third-party help to carry out blog-related tasks including design and technical support.
- Page: A static page within a blog that does not form part of the blogging content. For example, an "about" or "contact" page.
- PageRank: An algorithm used by Google to rank websites in their search engine results.
- Page view: The loading of a single HTML page on the internet. Also known as page impression.
- Permalink: A permanent link to a specific article, document or forum entry.
- PHP: Hypertext Preprocessor. A scripting language designed to be used with HTML to create dynamic pages.
- Pillar content: Meaty (and usually tutorial or how-to style) content that has long-term appeal, that becomes the backbone of your blog and what it's about (such as this glossary!).
- Pinterest: A social-network/bookmarking website best described as an online vision board. May also be a valuable traffic-driver for bloggers who's post images have been added to the site.
- Platform: A blog platform is the software used to create and maintain a blog.

- Plugin: In WordPress, a plugin is folder of files added to the blog in order to give it extra functionality or features.
- PNG: Portable Network Graphics. An image file type that unlike JPG doesn't lose quality when editing, but also does't support animation like GIFs do.
- Podcast: A digital file available for downloading to a media player (such as an iPod) or computer.
- Pop-ups: A form of online advertising displayed in a smaller window that appears upon visiting a site, or performing an action (such as submitting details). May include an ad, encouragement to sign up for a newsletter or enter a competition.
- Post: An article on a blog
- PPC: Pay Per Click. An advertising model in which the advertiser pays a blog owner each time their ad is clicked on the blog.
- Quantcast: An analytics website that measures traffic along with audience demographics, traffic and geography.

- Quora: A Q&A style website that aims to connect people via their interests, and lets you follow certain topics.
- Rate card: A document or web page that outlines the pricing and placement options of advertising opportunities on a blog and its related properties, such as newsletters.
- Reblog: To repost content from one blogger's post into your own blog, usually performed by simply clicking a "reblog" button, and indicated with a credit of sorts.
- Reciprocal link: An agreement between two bloggers to link to one another's blogs, performed to benefit each site's traffic.
- Rectangle: The name for a popular-sized website advertisement that's 180 pixels wide by 150 pixels high.
- Redirect: To force a website browser from one URL to another.
- Repin: The act of adding an existing Pinterest image, pinned by someone you follow, to one of your Pinterest boards and sharing it with your followers.
- Responsive design: Refers to a blog theme or website layout that changes in response to the size of the screen or device it's being viewed on.
- Retweet: The process of one Twitter user sharing the content (tweet) with their own audience by reposting it.
- Rich-media ads: Advertisements that may be interactive and may HTML, Flash or video.
- RSS: Stands for Rich Site Summary (and also Really Simple Syndication). It's a format (feed) for delivering website and blog content via an RSS reader or aggregator.

- RSS reader: A website or application that allows you to read the RSS feeds you've subscribed to in one place.
- Robots.txt: A file on your web server that tells search engines which blog content they should ignore.
- Self-hosted blog: A blog that requires the owner to purchase their own hosting services in order to use it. WordPress.org blogs are self-hosted, WordPress.com blogs are not.
- SEO: Search Engine Optimization. Techniques used to improve the visibility of a website within search results in order to increase site traffic.
- SERP: Search Engines Results Page. The list of web pages returned by a search engine as a result of the word or phrase being searched for.
- Shortcode: A short WordPress-specific code that can be used to quickly and easily embed pieces of content, files or objects.
- Sidebar: A column used to display content on a blog, other than the post or page's main content. For example: newsletter sign-up forms and advertisements.
- Site map: A list of pages on a website or blog that are accessible by visitors and search-engines. Like a table of contents.
- Slug: Keywords that describe a post or page (usually found in the title) and are used to form a URL.
- Social media: Websites (including blogs) and applications that encourage users to create, share and discuss content.
- Social network: A platform or website that focuses on connecting those with similar interests. Users typically have a profile, and are encouraged to interact with one another.
- Spam: Unsolicited advertising in the form of e-mails, blog comments, etc.
- Split testing: See A/B testing.
- Splog: A spam blog. Usually created with the purpose of improving the search-engine of the owner's other websites, to sell text-link ads, and/or, promote affiliate links. Content is typically poorly written or stolen.
- Sponsored post: A blog post that's paid for by a sponsor. Usually written by the blogger in their tone and style, and approved by sponsor. See also: Advertorial.
- StumbleUpon: A social-bookmarking website, that can drive traffic to website pages that have been submitted. Users "stumble" to find internet content related to their interests.
- Subscriber: A person who has chosen to stay updated on your latest blog posts via RSS.

- Su.pr: The little brother of StumbleUpon, Su.pr acts as a way of shortening URLs, submitting them to StumbleUpon, tracking their stats and sharing on Twitter – all from one location.
- SWF: Shockwave Flash. A type of file designed to deliver vector graphics, text, video, and sound over the internet.
- Tag: A word or name that classifies a blog post similar to a category, though usually more specific.
- Tag cloud: A collection of the words used to create post tags. Usually displayed in the sidebar in a manner that shows which has been used on the blog the most.
- Tagline: A short phrase or sentence, like a slogan, describing your blog. For example: "The stylish guide to blogging".
- Taxonomy: Classification of pages, posts and custom post types on a WordPress blog into categories, tags and link categories.
- Technorati: A blog search engine and directory. Also considered an authority on the state of the blogosphere.
- Text editor: A program that edits files in plain text format.
- Text link ads: Ads that consist of hyperlinked text. It's purchased by advertisers with the intention of improving the search engine ranking position of the page the ad links to.
- Theme: Files that modify the way a blog is displayed, like a "skin".
- Time on site/Time online: The amount of time a visitor spends on your blog.
- Timestamp: The date and time attached to digital data, such as a blog post or photo.
- Tool bar: An area of your screen at the top or bottom that contains useful info such as login links, sharing icons, and other features.
- Trackback: A method of notifying a blogger that another blogger has written something about their blog post and linked to it.
- Troll: Someone who leaves negative or hurtful comments on blog posts, usually in an anonymous fashion.
- Tumblr: A blogging platform, with features that encourage easy posting and reblogging.
- Tweet up: An event organized on Twitter for people to meet up in real life.
- Twitter: A microblogging platform. All posts (AKA "tweets") are 140 characters or less.
- Twitter client: A desktop or mobile application designed to help Twitter users manage their accounts.
- Twitter party: A virtual party, using the microblog, Twitter. Participants use a a pre-selected hashtag to chat with other attendees on a specific topic.

- UGC: User Generated Content. Posts or articles created by your visitors, and not you (the blog owner).
- Unique visitors: An analytics term that represents the number of visitors who visited your site during a certain time frame. Differs from visits in that the visitor is only counted once.
- URL: A Uniform Resource Locator (URL). The full address that identifies an exact location on the internet, includes all the colons and slashes.
- URL shortener: A tool that creates a shortened version of a URL.
- Users:In sites such as WordPress and Google Analytics, a user is a person who's been given access to an account.
- Viral: Content, such as posts, photos and videos, that is popular and quickly shared on the internet.
- Vlog: A video blog.
- Webinar: An online seminar, workshop or presentation. Related list:
- Weblog: A web log, also known as a blog. See blog.
- Web server: A computer containing software for hosting a website. Wide skyscraper: The name for a popular-sized website advertisement that's 160 pixels wide by 600 pixels high.
- Widget: A tool or content you can add to your blog's sidebar, such as a calendar, list of pages or archives menu.
- WordPress: An open-source (free) content management system, used to create customizable blogs and websites using themes and plugins.
- WordPress Multisite: A WordPress mode that allows you to create a network of multiple WordPress sites that run on a single installation of WordPress.
- WYSIWYG: Stands for What You See Is What You Get. This refers to what's being displayed in your post editor corresponding with what appears when the post is published.
- XHTML: Extensible HyperText Markup Language. Considered a "stricter" version of HTML.
- XML: Extensible Markup Language. Designed to transport and store data, where as HTML was designed to display data.
- YouTube: A Google-owned social video-sharing platform.

Conclusion

Social media marketing can wear all the hats of your business. It can increase sales, decrease customer service costs, acquire new customers, increase brand recognition, and more. It can influence nearly every aspect of your business. You simply have to condition it to do so.

Before you get into learning how to leverage social media to start increasing business profit we must first identify one thing: What Does Successful Social Media Look Like?

When you are starting a social media campaign, what are you thinking about? How to reach 20,000 fans, followers, or connections? Maybe even a more modest 1,000? That type of thinking won't get you very far.

Social media success is not about how many fans or followers you can get. Take a minute and let that register. Let it sink in, and always keep it in mind.

Instead of counting followers, try to think about how much engagement you are getting from the followers you already have.

When your customers are engaged, and willing to spread the word about your company, additional fans and followers will inevitably join in.

Like any aspect of marketing, social media marketing requires direction, a game plan, a blue print, a flow chart, whatever you want to call it...*you will need one.*

The objective is to map out your path to get from point A to B.

The marketing strategies outlined in this guide have been developed over 8 years of analyzing data. They are simple and intuitive. Best of all, they work!

The process may seem daunting at first, but give it a try and you will find it isn't as difficult as it seems. In fact, after getting familiar with the process, you can do it almost subconsciously while setting up your campaign. Each campaign can take you as little as the time it takes to click in and type your posts.

The Process

1. **Develop your campaign objective**: The objective should be narrow and focused. A reasonable goal would be to engage customers in order to increase brand awareness. An unreasonable goal would be to increase sales and increase customer satisfaction.
2. **Choose the right medium(s) for your campaign**: Unfortunately, this part takes some trial and error. Fortunately, many larger companies have done the leg work for you. It will take some time to get to know your audience in each medium, so just bear with it.
3. **Produce quality content**: CONTENT IS KING. There are massive amounts of posts and tweets being thrown at a single user at any given time. So, it is important that your posts not only get noticed, but you make them count and they make users *want* to read them (and share them).
4. **Set up a Content Management System / monitor your data**.
5. **Revise and repeat**: Measure and monitor your activities. Calculate your Return on Investment, analyze the data and look at where you need improvement in your company. Treat this as you would any other implementation within your company.

For more information on any of these topics please visit my website VCoppes.com or email me VCoppes@me.com!

www.ingramcontent.com/pod-product-compliance
Lightning Source LLC
Chambersburg PA
CBHW060206060326
40690CB00018B/4278